DAVID BRIGGS was born in 19:
Forest. He received an Eric Greg
published three previous collectior
Method Men, and *Cracked Skul*
David was co-editor of the Bristol-._____ ,   . .

DAVID BRIGGS

The Odyssey Complex
and Other Poems

CROMER

PUBLISHED BY SALT PUBLISHING 2024

2 4 6 8 10 9 7 5 3 1

Copyright © David Briggs 2024

David Briggs has asserted his right under the Copyright, Designs and
Patents Act 1988 to be identified as the author of this work.

First published in Great Britain in 2024 by
Salt Publishing Ltd
12 Norwich Road, Cromer, NR27 0AX United Kingdom
www.saltpublishing.com

Salt Publishing Limited Reg. No. 5293401

A CIP catalogue record for this book is available from the British Library

ISBN 978 1 78463 330 1 (Paperback edition)

Typeset in Sabon by Salt Publishing

Printed and bound in Great Britain by Clays Ltd, Elcograf S.p.A

Or you will rise and set your lines to work
With sadder joy but steadier elation.

DEREK WALCOTT, 'Nearing Forty'

Contents

THE ODYSSEY COMPLEX
AND OTHER POEMS

The Odyssey Complex

I

A sea of diamonds cut by sunlight and wind.
Sails on the horizon inch closer each second

and they're heading for his door. What can he do
to outwit the Achaean pressgang? His analyst helps

him to reject the *socially-normative assumptions
of goal-oriented adulthood* – the bullshit obsessions

with ambition, with status, with aspiring to
the bourgeois, masculine style of dudes

in 1990s automobile advertisements. He sees
the sequela – the years of bewildered aftermath

that follow for those who identify too strongly
with conventional nonsense about success. So,

to feign madness, he grabs his infant son,
sets him in a furrow and straps into a plough.

II

But the pressgang isn't fooled, and having been
co-opted he finds he's good at war. He accrues

the spoils – the ear of a king; the hard body
of a different slave, each night, in his truckle bed;

respectful salutations from famous men.
If they can sack this city, avenge the cuckold,

stuff their ships with gold – he won't be the worse
for a few years in the field. Easy to pick up

where he left off, since richer, with better stories.
And Penelope? She'll be relieved he's done as others.

Soon enough he'll be tending his vines again,
hunting with Argos, learning the balalaika.

Those old-school Jungians had life's phases pegged.
Only a few hard yards through this Trojan dust.

III

Uncanny, how it catches him right here –
in the orange light cast by flaming towers,

bloodwet thugs backslapping him as they lurch
on to murder and pillage – this equidistance

from the antipodes of youth and age. If the past
is a fertile valley the old yearn to revisit,

the future a floodplain imagined with equal ardour
by the young, birth and death the coasts

that bound them, right now he is poised, upright,
on the ridge between, drawn towards neither,

easy in his skin. Everything stills a beat,
and in the silence he knows himself to be

in the exact middle of his life. And then,
seconds later, to have passed that exact middle.

IV

What need for the foul stench of the *nekyia*,
for blood, fire, the conjuration of spirits,

since to have crossed life's silent meridian
is to be haunted daily by those good dead

we've outlived – by parents, friends, what-might-
have-beens had the world not gone so awry,

had our efforts been more strenuous. When
the route forward has become a cul de sac,

the mind makes its inevitable pivot to the past.
Still, his mother's spirit flickers, like Princess Leia

in R2D2's projector beam, but he's not hearing
what she's saying, is conscious only of this headwind

from the Underworld. When your parents die
nobody's standing between you and the grave.

V

So Odysseus, on the journey back to Ithaca,
to wife, son, throne, reconceives his goal

as a Freudian ego ideal he's often glimpsed:
hospitable king, secure, superannuated, trophies

hanging neatly on the wall – a version of himself
from which he's been endlessly diverted. He yearns,

in the midst of these bewildering years, not to be
the one reliant on the generosity of strangers

but the one toasting his guests in a fine palace
opening to an olive grove, a vineyard, the sea.

Now, among the Phaeacians, he tells more lies
of monsters, cannibals, lotus-addled hippies.

Self-conscious as hell about the absence of his crew.
Determined to be the author of his story.

στοργή
(storge)

Daughter

Lennox-Gastaut syndrome is the most common type of intractable
childhood epilepsy.
BRITISH EPILEPSY ASSOCIATION

She fell into the world as from a treetop –
a nest of speckled eggs spinning

in the certain drop through cracked air.
Incipient in her brain, the cuckoo

that would hatch, feed and grow
yet never fledge – Lennox Gastaut.

Today she will be 24
and I will remain grateful for

days when she can summon more
than her usual handful of words,

walk unaided across stain-proof carpet
and out into an institutional garden.

She fell out of my mind like a misplaced word;
there's no saying her again into rightness.

Was there more I could've done? For sure.
We do what we can without capsizing ourselves,

these lives we sail in her wake.
We secure our own lifejackets first.

Some days she barely knows who we are,
nor that we love her, or how;

that the name of our boat is Salvage.

On Visiting My Adult Daughter
at Her New Care Home

I

I watch you in your orthopaedic wheelchair
as the holiday-let houseboats tump by
on a stretch of the Thames at the end
of your care home garden. The August sun knows
nothing of epilepsy. It burns without a why,
whether you're alert or briefly unaware
of anything: houseboats, sun, the nurse who tends
to your tube with saline. Where do you 'go'?
Some ward of the mind's strip-lit corridor?
Better to think you just fall through a trapdoor
into still-favoured picture books: wolf-suited Max
on his private boat; a tiger drinking all Daddy's beer.
We call. You startle. Something comes clear,
though it's harder, these days, to bring you back.

II

Harder these days, I think, to explain,
as we check in at the LFT station,
then follow our escort to the Wessex Wing's
high dependency corridor, down which we troop
past tv-loud rooms – dementia patients
gently becalmed by *Singing in the Rain*,
or *Brief Encounter*. What was I expecting?
Kindly grandmas at jigsaws before Book Group
with a smile and a nod when you're wheeled in?
Many here don't know if it's dawn or evening,
let alone that you're among them indefinitely,
have needs so profound we accept *this* is home.
Then someone's screaming to be left alone
and we're less reassured than we'd hoped to be.

III

I'm less reassuring than I'd hoped to be
when I later tell Grandma on the phone.
But I'm probably projecting my own chagrin
at the limitations of your new home. I do
think it's fine. I've seen that you're known
and cared for – have kind hearts for company.
Child-minded ward of the state, ask anything!
Those dreams you can dream may be granted you –
trips on a Thames boat; *Frozen* on grey afternoons;
a bath with disco lights and show tunes;
someone to gently brush and plait your hair.
We're two islands of the infinitive "to be"
telegraphing *The Tiger Who Came to Tea* –
for twenty years our Book of Common Prayer.

IV

Twenty years of *Tiger* – our Book of Common Prayer,
a catechism over Skype at the Compline hour.
I call, you respond; a duet made of hemistichs
that we run through in declarative mood:
And then did they behold | *a big, stripy tiger* . . .
And greedily did that tiger | *drink all Daddy's beer* . . .
Meet it was they did feast | *on sausages and chips* . . .
And unto themselves bestowed | *a big tin of tiger food.*
It's never palled. Your only bedtime request.
A story doing repeatedly what stories do best:
delaying, then providing, the satisfaction felt
on the neat completion of a structural design.
Flashing on your inward eye, a tiger of the mind
tame in a kitchen, your fingers in his pelt.

V

Tame in a kitchen, your fingers in his pelt,
but having slaked his thirst he turns to bid
farewell, and leaves. And he won't call twice.
I always cue that final phrase for you:
. . . should come to tea again | *but he never did.*
Then, exchanging the hand you've been dealt,
you swap out Kerr for Sendak – a neat device
that turns the closure of Sophie's last adieu
into a trope of waiting, of *when* instead of *not.*
Replace . . . *he never did* with . . . *and it was still hot*
and intransigent departure becomes
rich with possibility, for as long as tea
stays hot, even if it's the lover's fate to be
the one who waits – to be of the patient ones.

VI

To be the one who waits – of the patient ones –
is more than I can take sometimes, not least
because I know what I'm waiting for won't be.
Our repetitious chat's hardened into ritual
and all faint hope of adult talk has ceased.
We'll never argue Zadie Smith v. Franzen
for best first novel, not Hughes versus Heaney,
Eliot over Dickens, Stones versus Beatles.
You'll never ask why I'm fond of autumn,
peer into my past, ask how I met your mum,
and why we didn't last. Such things are academic
now. The only one for whom they might
have mattered can neither read nor write.
We're frozen – in limbo more than relationship.

VII

Frozen – in limbo more than relationship –
and it's not pessimistic to expect
very little more. It's just what is, will be.
And at least it's a well-furnished limbo
where you'll meet neither cruelty nor neglect;
where you've learned and perfected the trick
of living without assumptions or anxiety –
untroubled by what you do or don't know.
It's time. We blow a kiss and say goodbye.
The August sun's sinking in a mackerel sky.
Jane thanks the nurse for plaiting your hair
and we're off, back out along the corridor
to the car. From a window on the first-floor,
you're waving adieu in your wheelchair.

On The Pequod
after Dan Beachy-Quick

And just as words contain
the distance they express
      between themselves
          and the things they name,
so Ahab's whalebone leg
occupies the space
his severed leg once held.
And lying in his hammock
listening to the Pequod
pitch and creak, with nothing
but empty space adjacent
to his one vestigial leg,
he notes the seeming presence
of a phantom leg that feels
      more material than any leg
          of flesh or whalebone made,
but isn't fooled. Ahab knows
this 'leg' is just a nothing,
is just a word that now contains
the distance it expresses
      between itself
          and the thing it names.

My daughter lives beyond me,
epileptic, nil by mouth,
      in an institution several
          counties far from here,
and we communicate by Skype,
and I read the same picture books

we've shared these twenty years;
and just as this routine's become
            the sum of our relationship,
                        seems almost to define it,
it does so now in such a way
that this vague word 'relationship'
seems mostly to contain
the distance it expresses
            between itself
                        and the thing it names.

And Tashtego fell headfirst
into the Heidelburgh Tun –
            that's Ishamel's ludic phrase
                        for a sperm whale's severed head,
brimful with spermaceti,
that whalers have cracked open
like a Brinksmat bankvault –
a whalehead that itself then slipped
its starboard ropes to fall headfirst
            into the South Pacific,
                        Tashtego wombed within.
And it would've borne him plumb down to
the briny depths, if Queequeg
hadn't dived right in to rescue him,
to pull Tashtego breach-born from
that brine-soaked whale's head tomb.
            Or womb. And some
                        might call this 'rebirth' –
a word that for a moment

contains not just Tashtego
(and hope for almost all of us)
but the distance it expresses
        between itself
                and the thing it names.

νόστος

(nostos)

Crackle (A-Side)

In memoriam Mark Fisher

Friday night. Mix Manhattans.
Put on the record I've bought.
       Bourbon, vermouth, Talking Heads –
       just three of many kindred pills
       and soft-edged analgesics
            I've come now to rely on.
Addict of the hi-fi,
       the gentle whump of needle
       touching down on sounding strip,
       vinyl's haunting crackle –
            sound of power cuts and post-punk,
            of trying out new hairstyles.

Why this nostalgia
for the granular, analogue world?
       Is it that I'm haunted
            by the ghost of that utopia
            I'd been fool enough to think
            was almost in our grasp?
Once, it seemed, there'd be no end
to maintenance grants, free degrees,
       poets on Parkinson,
            public libraries.
And a better future beckoned –
       egalitarian technology,
            in every town a world-class orchestra,
               council homes to rival even
               Vienna's Wohnpark Alterlaa.
Before the demolition of the post-war high-rise dream.

A record's grooves fill with dust.
      When spun, its crackle makes
      the weather in a room.
Briefly, post-millennium, some bands in post-production
added crackle in the studio.
          Is it mere indulgence now
          to slide one from its sleeve,
               this liquorice-black flat earth
               between forefinger and thumb?
Not everyone is casting wistful glances back.
Some things have improved.
      Some ideas survive.

Marconi thought no sound was lost:
no word, no note, no scream.
      That sound, once made, never dies,
      just sinks beneath our human pitch –
          the world, therefore, an echo vault
          of ever-fainter soundwaves.
And he hoped one day to fashion
      alchemical devices
          able to re-amplify
               these currently inaudible
               yet stubborn sonic ghosts.
Marconi dreamed he'd one day hear
      the actual voice of Jesus preach
      the Sermon on the Mount.

Hard to lose anything now,

even if we want to.
Digital's made sure of that.
    The only thing that we've lost's
    the certainty of loss.
Unless we can be said to have lost what never existed,
be haunted by a might have been.
So I sometimes think –
    Mr Analogue Nostalgia –
    living out my quaint routines:
        crate-digging in record shops
        on Fridays after work,
            refusing still to use or own
            a hashtag or a smartphone.
Between the needle landing
    and the first track's opening bars . . .
        as though the neoliberals hadn't won.
Each night, I put a record on.

Crackle (B-side)

I

ECHOING DERRIDA, Mark Fisher describes hauntology, a near homophone for ontology, as the agency of the virtual – of elements that are not supernatural, but which nonetheless act without existing. A hauntological element is a virtuality whose threatened coming is already playing a part in undermining the present state of things. The spectre of Communism Marx and Engels saw haunting Europe even before Communism itself became corporeal. Or the way anxiety about the act of composition haunts each poem's particular failure (which, of course, includes this poem).

The progressive popular modernity of the post-1945 settlement informed the milieu in which Fisher and his generation spent our youth – we imagined a future utopia of egalitarian technology, of enfranchisement into creative expression; we dreamed of liberation from tedious labour and economic precarity.

But this portal that was briefly propped open during the post-war decades was subsequently closed by successive neoliberal governments from 1979.

Francis Fukuyama asserted 'the end of history'.

We found ourselves inhabiting a future very different from the one we'd imagined.

We learned that it's also possible to be haunted by the spectre of an imagined future that never came to be – to be spooked by a virtuality whose thwarted incipience is now playing a part in undermining our acceptance of the present state of things.

II

THE REMOVAL of maintenance grants, social housing, low rents, and protected tenancies exerts an effect on cultural production. Increasing precarity makes it ever more important for makers working in the arts to achieve economic security at pace, and this tends to result in a reliance on formulaic tropes. It leads to the production of that which one can be confident will sell, rather than to formal and structural experimentation. The process of marketisation exacerbates a tendency to turn out cultural productions that resemble what is already successful.

If there's one factor above all else which contributes to cultural conservatism, it is the vast inflation of the cost of rents and mortgages.

III

CULTURAL CONSERVATISM buttresses a position that Fredric Jameson refers to as the nostalgia mode, a mode especially dominant in early twenty-first century Western culture – cue Mark Ronson's production of the Amy Winehouse single 'Valerie', with its employment of modern studio technology to ape an idea of 1960s soul, a sound that belongs neither to the present nor to the past but to an implied timeless era. An eternal 1960s.

The retro-maniacal nostalgia mode, seen everywhere in contemporary culture – in fashion, in popular music, in nostalgic tv dramas, in the taste among well-heeled 40-somethings for mid-century Scandinavian furniture – has caused a waning of historicity, just as the neoliberal destruction of communitarian solidarity, as well as of ordinary people's economic security, has created a compensatory hungering for the well-established and the familiar.

Dyschronia characterises the processes of late capitalism.

Endless recycling and collage of old tropes.

In other words, the future has been cancelled.

IV

HAUNTOLOGICAL POPULAR MUSIC is music suffused with an overwhelming melancholy. Its principal sonic signature is crackle, the surface noise made by dust in the grooves of a vinyl record, which, in the late 1990s to early 2000s, was added to tracks digitally, in the studio, by artists like Portishead and Burial.

Crackle manifests as soundwaves, and as such it can be said to exist, whether its origin is dust or a digitally applied effect. But what it expresses, and what it activates, is a yearning for an older regime of materiality.

For a certain generation it serves as a memory bridge to a pre-digital age in which the relentless march of neoliberalism seemed less certain and socio-economic conditions enabled a Modernist spirit of formal and structural experimentation.

Did that regime actually exist as imagined?

Is it merely a nostalgic projection?

Either way, for some, the very idea of that regime manifests like a ghost whenever a stylus hits a record's groove. And that ghost can act upon a subject without necessarily needing to exist.

It is hauntological.

V

TO READ the melancholia of crackle through a Jungian notion of libido is to differentiate it from mourning. In mourning, libido is slowly and painfully withdrawn from the lost object. In melancholia, libido remains attached to what has disappeared.

And libido may even remain attached to what never existed – to lost visions of the future featuring ever increasing democratisation of the initially elitist Modernist project.

Social housing inspired by Le Corbusier.

Higher education maintenance grants.

Well-funded libraries.

The BBC's Radiophonic Workshop.

The music of punk and post-punk.

Universal basic income.

Listen to crackle and hear therein the muttering ghosts of progressive popular modernity. Hear them lament the supplanting of bespoke structures suited to the zeitgeist by tropes co-opted from works of the past as part of a nakedly commercial agenda.

You may feel like an outcast among the cultural productions of your time.

OTHER VOICES argue that things have become more egalitarian during the last forty years. They suggest that you ask a range of non-cis, -het, -white artists if they would rather return to the so-called progressive popular modernism of the 1960s and 1970s or continue to develop their careers in the present moment, despite the neoliberal hegemony.

Not everything, including the attitudes and profiles of cultural gatekeepers, has become less progressive, they say.

They ask if I really want to assert there's less formal innovation in the arts, or even in popular music, than during earlier decades.

They doubt it's tenable to argue that dyschronia and the business-like appropriation of stylistic tropes from the past is a phenomenon peculiar only to artists working in a late capitalist context.

And I concede.

They make a strong case.

The hauntology of vinyl crackle can sometimes sound like the manifesto of a left-leaning midlife dissatisfaction. Spend as much time as I do in record-shops, and it can feel like a distinctive feature of midlife nostalgia.

And yet, there's something about that dust-flecked crackle between the needle landing and the opening bars.

It's hauntological – a conjuration.

Enter the ghosts of my past and historical future.

Spirals

I've lived so long in this westering town
any day's routine might take me down
streets I've walked a thousand times.

I pass through the same points
in space, just one rotation
farther out in time each time –

so many unspooling spirals.
King's Road, Clifton. Buying
corn tortillas from the Mexican deli.

A hot day in July. Can it really be
twenty-five years ago I stood here
with N., before the divorce,

imagining a propitious future
as we glimpsed our reflections
in a window display for furniture

and fancy interiors. Fifteen since
I met R. at that bar on the corner
to get his notes on my first MS?

And what happened to K.,
that barrister who loved am-dram
and dreamed of playing Hamlet?

Every street's haunted.
Even the one we live on now.
I walked it often in a former life,

before I knew you, before you
salvaged me from the roadside skip
of my first quarter century.

And when the night is cool,
the voices of twentysomethings,
passing our garden for the park,

inked to the neck, with take outs
and worries about money,
seem as atavistic and unceasing

as the suck of surf on Dover beach.
To stand among roses and honeysuckle,
hearing them, proffers a rare chance

at a satisfying style of stillness.
As when you stop suddenly
mid dervish spin and feel the earth

continue to carousel around you –
know that you've become
the one unmoving thing
in the whole spiralling cosmos.

Static

"There is no time here. Not any more."
SAPPHIRE AND STEEL

I sat on an acrylic rug   in a mustardbrown front room
watching static on tv   for much of the 1970s   the dizzying swell
of silvered-flecks on a black screen   like an ocean at night   and me
a whaler at the masthead   scranning whaleless seas   for spoutings
tailfins   flukes   before the Hersee test card
in the midst of power cuts   before channels spawned like kelp
staring into tv static   for hours with the sound up
the landscapes of my childish mind   formed like archipelagos
in vast pre-Cambrian seas   what was it I was hunting in
the Big Bang's echo?   in those rumblings of the universe
humming through cold space   and cast by cathode-ray tube onto
inter-schedule screens?   little Ahab with his telescope
hunting down his nemesis   way back before the decades got locked in
endless feedback loops   of retro kitsch   of vintage
before the "end of history"   but tv static's no pop icon
foregrounded as signifier   for 70s period detail
it's no homely pack of Ajax   in *A Very English Scandal*
no orange Raleigh Chopper   on a street in *Life on Mars*
no BBC2 ident   no *Beano*   no space hopper
and what does it evoke now?   having time to waste I guess
or the tantalising prospect   of something good to come
which never came   but haunts me still
melancholic afterglow   of my generation's hope
which hadn't   then   been cancelled

Oak Galls

The future I wanted did not materialise.
Truer to say it was cancelled;

a future I thought had been well planted,
a sapling shaking out its limbs into leaf;

a future conceived in the shadow of oaks
that grew in front of my childhood home;

oaks I hid behind, or broke cover from only
to hurl a mad volley of hard green grenades

in acorn wars fought between 7-year-olds;
oaks I climbed, in whose branches I sat

escaping the sadness of home;
oaks supplying the oak galls from which

I fermented this ink I'm writing in now
of a future I no longer think possible, but which

I glimpsed once, through high summer leaves
of oaks who've swelled mere inches since then

and no doubt will outsurvive all of us
in a future that I hope will be inherited

by a gentler, more patient species –
mindful, more constant than mine.

The Flea Market

smells of mid-century chests of drawers
and joss-sticks; is chock full of stuff the zeitgeisty
majority have deemed worthless – a purgatory

for the obsolescent, the rejects tossed aside
by Progress on his single-minded march to the future.
But the feather boa on that mannequin, there,

once shimmered with promise in the mirror
of a suburban boy in 60s Totterdown playing
air-guitar to *Axis: Bold as Love.* That cocktail

cabinet in formica and glass, with pineapple
ice-bucket, played host to fabulous parties
in a 70s newbuild, where X met Y and kissed.

What do we really know of a pair of binoculars?
A set of sherry glasses? A tin toy fire engine?
Something inheres, radiates from their surfaces.

Things have history. For someone, once,
they mattered. Now, they've passed their meridian –
they sit out the remainder in a Gloucester Road

flea market, hearing the slow tick of entropy,
hoping while there's time still to be picked
and pitched back into anyone's narrative.

ἐναντίοςδρόμος
(enantiodromia)

The Difference

He had to acknowledge it was true: each passing second
     now, at 48, seemed to constitute a vanishingly
smaller proportion of his mortal jaunt than it had
     thirty years earlier. Time was accelerating
with each passing year – a trick of perspective
     that partly explained the smug grin of satisfaction
on the creaseless face of his 18-year-old self
     in the photographs he'd just unearthed.

But what that time-rich youth couldn't know,
     he soliloquised, as he sat archiving the past
over a nice little '98 Saint Veran, is that now I bring
     to each and every moment of my 40-something existence
an additional thirty years of experience – accumulation
     of life's sediment; thick palimpsest of well-read interiority.
And this enables me to savour every second like
     a sommelier in some fancy gaff, to taste in each experience
the gillyflowers that grew alongside it while rain's
     perfumes rose from loamy soil.

These half-convincing consolations of age – the retired magician
     pulling a rabbit from under his bar stool;
the defeated champion returning to the solitude
     of his trophy room; the politician steering his answer
towards the question he believes will make the difference.

Simian

The gorilla is dandling his feet in the moat
surrounding Gorilla Island, telling a crowd
of zoo-goers about his deepening midlife crisis.

For a post-Jungian (which is how he identifies)
the 'midlife crisis' is clearly more plausible as
psycho-social construct than biological inevitability,

but life on Gorilla Island being what it is –
the pressure to sustain his alpha male status,
combined with a growing conviction that

the last ten years might've been better spent
writing poetry than fighting for supremacy –
the nagging doubts have become harder to ignore.

He's just not feeling it anymore. The thought
of having to fulfil his duties even another month
fills him with dread and ennui. Why did he think

an unlimited choice of breeding partner
the be-all and end-all? Most of his progeny
are just waiting for their moment to drown him

in the moat, while former mates, freed now
from the obligations of motherhood,
are taking influential roles in simian political life

and enjoying a post-menopausal renaissance.
All he wants is to retire to his hammock
clutching a bunch of memories
and bananas.

Little Red Cap

ROSETTA: . . . may our luck find the
                  Regressive road to Grandmother's House.
                      from *The Age of Anxiety*, by W. H. AUDEN

After she'd shot Grandma between those great big eyes,
as the pistol-smoke cleared, she realized. How strange!
They were three aspects of the same psyche –

the old woman, her mother, herself . . . three faces
showing the phases of just one woman's story:
virgin-mother-crone. That desire-line she'd followed

through lupine woods had been no more real than weather
in a bad novel, had actually been her life's journey
from youth to age. She looked at the pistol.

Whose were these liver-spotted hands?
Whose was this shallow, timorous breathing?
This sense of having neglected something important?

She grappled the bedclothes against the cold.
Perhaps she was not, after all, the protagonist?
Might she and Grandma have been avatars all along?

Visions in the mind of a mother caught between youth
and the kind of old woman she wished to become?
In the midst of this uncanny cognizance, a girl

she barely recognized had appeared, silhouetted
by weak sunlight streaming through the doorjamb.
In one hand a basket of provisions. In the other, a pistol

with just one silver bullet in the chamber.

Transitions

Leaving the gallery, you and I fell
into typical mini-break chat –
how we'd throw it all in tomorrow,
and move here to Penzance,
live on our wits, write and paint
looking out on Gwavas Lake.
I mentioned K., a poet I'd met
a few times at readings in London,
who'd just upped and left one day
for Penzance (or was it Falmouth?)
some years back and might well
be living here still.
                    Seconds after,
who should appear on Victoria Place,
typically fabulous, in starched denim
with milk-white bracebuttons,
rockabilly bouffant pinned at one side
with a red rose hair-clip, but K. herself.
As though I'd conjured her.
K. for real, floating zephyr-like
on Penzance air like Chagall's Bella
in *The Bouquet by the Window.*
K. in the flesh, heading to Newlyn
to run a workshop based
on a show called *Transitions.*
                    So we followed her,
and what should I find on a trellis table
but Eno's *Oblique Strategies,*
that occult series of prompts for artists,
and we're allowed to touch anything

[44]

so I cut the deck and my card reads:
Are there sections?
Consider the transitions.
A microphone pops. At the front,
flanked by an indeterminate object
rendered in construction-site plastic,
K. is being introduced and
      the words hurry
      intoeachother
         and then
         apart . . .
and now she is reading
      how she wrote across days
         and off the edge
            of the page

Living with the Douglases

Michael Douglas is renting our spare room
again. It's just temporary, till work picks up

and/or Catherine takes him back.
He's an early riser, and on bright mornings

we'll find him out in the garden with
black coffee and a Thai stick, looking

so much like Sandy Kominsky/Grady Tripp
we wonder how much acting was involved

in these recent projects. But it's still work I rate –
notwithstanding the acclaimed roles he played

in the 80s and 90s – since it feels
as though he's comfortable enough now

in his accomplishments to take himself
a little less seriously; as though he no longer needs

some Nietzschean hero narrative to flatter
an entitled sense of celebrity and is enjoying

the opportunity to play gently botched characters
with the (often unfulfilled) potential for redemption.

As though he's embraced his inner clown.
Sometimes, I wonder if it really is Michael Douglas

who's living with us, and my wife'll say, "Well,
if he's not Michael Douglas then who the hell is he?"

And I'll laugh and say: "You're right. I'm ridiculous.
Of course he's Michael Douglas," before knocking

to see if he wants a cup of joe. I like the way
he's arranged his flamboyant neck scarves

on his tailor's dummy and, sometimes, I think
Should I grow my hair out like Michael Douglas?

Whenever I encounter a crisis of self-doubt,
I'll give myself a pep talk, saying things like

"Michael Douglas may be going through
a tough patch right now, but he's got chutzpah

and is a pretty good style model for the older man."
But then I'll recall that much of his swagger,

the élan that enables him to carry off that look,
comes from years of Hollywood stardom

and a foot-locker of great anecdotes featuring
some of the world's most glamorous people.

And I'll realise with a sigh that my three books
with a small press and that time I shared the bill

with Don Paterson don't really compare,
that I'm probably kidding myself.

But then I say: "Fuck it. *I'm* Spartacus!" And laugh.
And my wife says, "That was *Kirk* Douglas, knucklehead."

Singing Along with Edith

When Edith Piaf takes on Thursday nights
at The Gallimaufry, our local bar, I think
'That's quite a come down.' But we go,

and she seems to enjoy the appreciation
of a small, musically literate crowd
that can't quite believe its luck.

It's even more surprising that she eschews
the late-style phase of reinvention; Edith sings
her hits and ends every set with *that* song.

I like to watch people in the crowd
as we accompany her. A pack of beery lads
wandering in off the street will belt it out,

spreading their arms in laissez-faire gestures,
nodding to each other, pointing at themselves
as though they're Frank Fucking Sinatra.

Entirely unaware that this one's a love song.
They're not even halfway through their mortal jaunts
I suppose, and that does make it easier

to give regret the finger, since it seems
there's nothing so banjaxed it can't be un-banjaxed
by the dedicated application of time and effort.

But it's generally an older crowd at The Gally,
with better French, and we sing with less swagger,
little trembling flickers of doubt in our eyes.

For all our enthusiasm we can't commit entirely
to the lyric. "Je ne regrette *rien*?" Really?
"Rien *de rien*?" Sceptical of our ability to redeem

every ill-advised choice from the past –
to turn a stumble into a quick-step flourish,
a bum note into a surprising jazz riff – we falter.

Love notwithstanding, time's running out.
Options are narrowing. But then, there's Edith.
You can feel the scar tissue in her voice.

And it's all the more impressive that despite
the troubles, the tragedies, *her* assertion of love
stands up to the end. An article of faith.

That's how we try to sing, Jane and me,
beaten but unbowed, from the gloom
at the back of the bar –

> *Non, je ne regrette rien,*
> *Car ma vie, car mes joies*
> *Aujourd'hui . . . ça commence avec toi!*

hoping it might be so.

Cinema One

It's not as if we don't try to understand
the blood-dimmed tide of history,
but the human span's insufficient.
      Bookended by millennia,
      poorly placed, we speculate.

Every one of us walks in
halfway through the movie
      clutching a bucket of popcorn,
      with plastic straws in noisy drinks,

arguing loudly about our seats
through essential dialogue,
leaving our crap in the footwell.
      It's over our heads.
      We leave before the credits.

All Flesh is Bluegrass

At seventeen, the Good Time
seemed always to be stuck
in gridlocked traffic
in the band's transit van,
with the drums and pedal steel,
while ahead at the venue
he slouched backstage
mindlessly noodling
on a Blueridge six-string,
and impatient booing
from the auditorium
flooded a draughty corridor.

Briefly in midlife he felt
master of his own time,
as though bass and drums
had found a tight lock;
the flatpicking rhythms
of subjective time
and of expectation
kept in perfect syncopation
with reality's 2/4 boom-chuck;
the spans of the concert
and of his stamina
were precisely equal.

It doesn't last. Soon the months
begin to slide past –
broken-off boughs in rapids
heading inexorably for the falls

while a juvenile banjo
duels with a vintage guitar –
a warning that he's
out of his element,
has maybe one last chance
to play the Grand Ole Opry
before someone pulls the plug
on the whole damn scene.

Praise

the Jesus freak is dancing
in the central reservation –
a vagabond itinerant

in broken shoes and raincoat,
his scurfy hi-vis gilet
proclaims JESUS SAVES in sharpie –

and his earbuds are aflame
with seraphimic tongues of fire
singing mid-Atlantic Jesus rock;

he's twirling like a dervish,
or an iPod advert silhouette,
as though there's no one watching

except Jesus, his placebo –
is he dancing to persuade us
of his inner joy's contagion?

is he wired? where's his foxhole?
does he have somewhere to lay his head?
have years of psychedelics

blown the wiring in his lightshow?
and should someone intervene?
No, the Jesus freak is happy;

let him shake his matted elflocks
in the central reservation
while commuters headache home;

let him telegraph the heterodox,
let him dance to please his inwit's god
beneath the April stillicide
of rainfall lit by headlamps

κατάβασις
(katabasis)

Cactus

Maybe it's the descent into my sunset years,
or the delayed afterburn of all that peyote
I necked as a kid, but so much of waking life

now is ambushed by reverie – unscheduled
little *nekyias* with ghosts from my past – I'm
barely here at all. I can be fully conscious of

that cactus on the windowsill, for example,
for little more than a second, before the thought
of how well it's growing will transport me

to former cacti in former kitchens –
to T. (who got eye cancer) planning his next
Situationist exploit on Exeter High Street,

while J. upcycles a washing-machine drum
into a coffee table, and M. (where's he now?)
reads *Lonely Planet* guides over a beer and a cigarette

and I guess that our landlord, that young Tory
(Kevin?), who seemed half-terrified each rent day,
has probably accrued more than enough wealth

by now to alleviate some of his nerves
(or compound them); and this was just before
my first marriage and all its windowsills

framing prickly arguments in Salisbury,
Oxford, Bristol; which was itself just before
I met Jane and became a real adult capable of caring

for houseplants . . . But then I'll come to –
find I'm in my dressing gown, in our kitchen,
blinking at a cactus, the kettle having boiled

I've no idea how long ago – and Jane
must be wondering (again) what's happened
to our cup of tea in bed.

Horses

in memoriam David Selwyn

Halfway through a weird trip, he stood at the fringe
of an unfamiliar wood, clutching a leather-bound book
bequeathed to him by a dead friend – a book that bristled

with life as he riffled its pages. Pictures emerged
into three dimensions from the flat plane of the page
like early vertebrates crawling from primordial ooze:

a picture of a moth flickered up from its gutter
and into the trees; a drawing of a spider abseiled
from the binding and scuttled into undergrowth.

He slammed it shut; a gust of wind from the covers
blew a whicker of sycamore leaves into his eyes.
Stranger yet, the book seemed to know where it was.

He heard it whisper: "We're here. Let us show you."
So he stepped in under the canopy, stood awhile
studying the title page, considering the path ahead,

saw that one was a perfect simulacrum of the other.
And as he walked, and as each bend revealed
a new vista of trees, ferns, toadstools, he turned

the pages in step, only to find corresponding images
forming on the paper in front of him like photographs
in developing fluid. The book was mapping the wood

in real time, as though perfectly in sympathy with it.
And sometimes predicting it – a diorama
of roe deer cantered across a page and off its edge,

only to be mirrored, seconds later, by actual deer
skittishly crossing the path and darting into bracken.
Such an intricate mechanism! He was entranced.

The final page showed a beech-tree cathedral
shot through with moonbeams. An eldritch space
in which was pictured an unbridled team

of horses – piebald, skewbald, dun, roan, jet –
their breath curling in midsummer starlight;
their brown eyes aflame. He looked up

to find himself right there. And as they came
nodding, the horses for real, he recalled
his friend's take on Swift's houyhynnms:

"The genius," he'd say, "was in making
those horses seem so rational, so civilised,
so *very nearly* convincing."

Genius Loci
in memoriam Roddy Lumsden

An empty carriage. Three stops to Farringdon.
I'm prepping my talk for a conference.
In the adjoining carriage, just one

other passenger, glimpsed askance
through the carriage-door windownook
as we swerve on bends in the line

charted to detour ancient plague pits.
Your profile. Your idiosyncrasies.
Eidetic hallucination? Could be.

Just me, the rattle of wheels on rail,
an ad for financial services neither
you nor I will ever have need of.

Past the ticket barrier into weak sun.
Streets paved with memories –
nights at The Betsey; M. or K. reading

from new books; you hosting –
mellifluous East Neuk brogue, twitchy blink,
that way you had of flipping recto╱

verso with one hand while clutching
a pint in the other. The pub's still going,
though you won't drink here again now.

And what brings me this way today
after too many years,
has nothing like enough to do

with friendship, or with poetry.

Cointreau

in memoriam Avril Henry

I love its boozy citrus hit,
how in licking my lips post-sip
it sharpens that extra-temporal bit
of self that's able to taste
the past in the present,
taste two moments co-eval
in its sweetness.
          And it puts me in mind of Avril
placing a bottle of Harpic, and Marigolds,
on the shelf to the side of her bathtub –
ever considerate of others,
of those who might find her
many days after –
and climbing in carefully
in her best purple kaftan;
diluting the poison
in a brandy-glass measure
of blood-orange Cointreau
to smother its foulness.
          And I like to imagine
that she had a book,
perhaps her translation
of Guillaume de Deguileville's
Pilgrimage of the Life of the Manhode,
from which I also imagine her
reading aloud while Death inched closer,
put one cold hand on her heart.
          There's just enough of the past
swilling around in the present,

like just enough barbiturate
in a terminal glass of Cointreau;
like there's just enough barbiturate
for the task, in a vial
she'd hidden so presciently
beneath floorboards,
fearful of interventions,
of untimely police raids,
of cold-calling journalists.
She taught me so much I'm grateful to know.
      Each year, on this day,
I pour for myself
a chilled, double rocks glass
                of Cointreau.

Sioux Shoes

There they are, on wall-mounted shoe trees
behind glass – sixteen pairs of Sioux shoes,
relics from the massacre of the Great Plains.

It's been forty years, but here I am again
at the American Museum near Bath,
mesmerized by the embroidered slippers,

the poignant headdress of eagle feathers.
Not the first time I've been kicked into
verse by ceremonial moccasins

behind museum glass – it happened once
before at the Royal Ontario Museum
and now again today

in a room I'm so sharply conscious
of having visited before I might
reach out for the hand of my eight-year-old self –

for we stand side-by-side, ghosted by time.
We're sure there was a railroad carriage
in the gardens. I have a photograph

somewhere, of me with another boy,
the son of a friend of my mother's who
must've driven us here all those years ago

and whose name I can't recall. Slouched
on that observation car in our flares
and cable-knit jumpers, fringed by camellias,

we're staring down the camera – a dutiful
pause in the packed schedule of eight-year-olds.
We're striking west in the great land grab.

I've recalled that day with a sepia-tinged
dissonance every time I've driven past
the museum sign. And I've lived down the road

for twenty-five years. So why have I waited
so long to return? After the main house,
a cafeteria hot dog, we walk the gardens

and I seek out the railroad carriage.
No one remembers it. And it's as though
I've been uncoupled from something. Later,

I'll rummage for the photograph
and it'll be as I recall, only I'd never noticed
the date stamp: SEP 1980.

The month my father was killed. So that was it.
Here I am again with the Sioux shoes.
My childhood and the Battle of Wounded Knee.
The deaths of Sitting Bull and my father.

Breath
for A.O.

the paleolithic cave painter poised
to blow crushed charcoal

from one hand through
the finger-stencil of the other

onto white limestone;
breath implicit

in the making of images
from the outset

once, I sat in a candlelit hall
while A. recited from memory

for an hour – flawless, flashes
of extempore composition,

her breath at times supplanting
the printed word

as though writing
on hand-pressed air

I've tried composing aloud
but the words condense

like breath mist momently –
will not hold their shape

mostly I sit in an airless room
with paper and ink – striving

beyond what I can write
towards what I hope to write

and breathing,
                    albeit heavily

Hemispheres

you may well ask
since what happened happened
in this jar on this shelf
like a pickled walnut
my neural complexity
the lifespan I might've expected
for abstract reasoning
a mature specimen of my type
my particular preferences
identity has weathered
made liquid as waves
do not believe the evangelists
their oasis is a mirage
institutional property
if whatever this is *is*
perhaps I am the clue to
consider a brain 'in a jar'
and in me you have perfected
whoever is dreaming

and the answer's yes
I've been whitening in formalin
in a university museum
from my measurements
I was about midway through
at the pith of my capacity
and linguistic expression
yet I cannot recall my name
the faces of those I loved
to a range of dunes
in the scirocco
of transhumanism or cryogenics
I am meat brain
an item in a catalogue
merely a simulation after all
ontological status
contemplating a brain in a jar
an instinct for mimesis
is dreaming whom

ξενία

(xenia)

Habitat
after W. H. Auden

I. THE DEATH OF ARCHITECTURE
(for Matthew Caley)

Are we to remain, to quote Gérard de Nerval's famous line,
beings whose "towers have been destroyed?"

GASTON BACHELARD

From Salisbury's spire and the Westminster gargoyles
    to Grenfell's flammable cladding
is almost one full turn of the millennial clock hand.
    What next, for our final century?
To dedicate a whole town's wealth to one monument,
    for the span of a human life,
while the carpenters and masons by whom it is raised
    squat around flickering fires
in single-room hovels on earth and stone floors, would be
    seen as unthinkable these days,
yet those with high stakes in the mad cult of property
    still crave conspicuous designs –
a Bond villain's eyrie on a north Devon clifftop;
    McCloud's neo-Modernist cuboids;
superfluous, art deco department-store buildings
    re-purposed by developers;
the golden sheath of Toronto's Trumpian tower
    reflecting the sun so fiercely
it melts the window-frames of neighbouring office-blocks.
    Adorno wrote that poetry,
post Holocaust, could not be other than barbaric.
    If we must build – homes first; then spires!

[75]

Most of us would settle for shelter, a dreaming nook
    for fertile laziness, as far
from a crime scene, an arterial road, a floodplain
    as our bank accounts will allow.
Just how many affordable homes for a Gherkin
    or Shard? For a Burj Khalifa?
A house is a means to inhabit the universe.
    A room is a true gestalt space.
Houses, like poems, are for those who live in them,
    not for those by whom they are built.

II. THANKSGIVING FOR A HABITAT
(for Jane Briggs)

Le monde bat de l'autre côté de ma porte.
PIERRE ALBERT BIROT, *Les amusements naturel*

Though sometimes I'll picture an art deco mansion
        on a cliff above sunbathing seals,
this Victorian semi in central Bristol
        feels palatial enough to me,

who started out on a 70s estate
        on the edge of a dull Hampshire town.
Turns out my own little breadcrumb trail
        didn't stretch so far after all,

but for one who chose meaningful work
        instead of the gold rush, who's laboured
in an obscure corner of the Inky Republic,
        it's enough to reduce me to tears.

Mature magnolia in the front garden
        and a spring-flowering crab out back;
Bathstone fronted, plantation shutters,
        bay window; four up, three down.

It doesn't flood. There's a park and shops.
        We've a study space each, you and me.
A side return, French windows that open
        each spring on a redbrick-walled garden.

Still, the world pulse beats beyond our door –
        coughs like gunshots in a bank queue,
dyspeptic men high on conspiracy.
        But most smile sweetly, keep the requisite distance

in the aisles of local supermarkets.
        Living here, we've been able to forget,
for a few selfish moments,
        the ventilators lined like dominoes

in ICUs across Europe, America, the world.
        But though we've not had symptoms
we've often slept poorly, spent the small hours
        making futile reckonings with eternity.

We've picked up dusty account books
        to realise our all-too-common mistake –
all along, the debts we owed each other
        we'd been chalking up to ourselves.

And in the Month of Inessential Chores
        I pruned the flowering crab apple,
laddered my way into topmost branches
        with a handsaw and secateurs

to thin out the dead wood and watershoots.
        A passing pigeon might fly through.
The view up there was novel –
        neighbouring gardens, a city made lucid

by months with less daily traffic.
        And it was hard to feel dystopian
in deckchairs, in unseasonal sunshine,
        so we flirted coyly with optimism,

rapt in the seeming proliferation
        of native birdsong, the unalloyed air.
We dreamed the Great Reconfiguration.
        And though we never quite succumbed

to the bourbon breakfast, the booze hour
        did click around earlier each day,
like ice cubes chinking in a glass of rosé.
        And there were so many ways to keep count:

that stack of empties by the bin;
        the dwindling stock of packets and tins;
the litany of household names
        falling into administration;

and the daily government briefing;
        while the Minister for Plague shoves aside
the count, leaning in with bonsai scissors
        to prune a perfectly manicured tree,

a border appears in the Irish Sea,
        floodwaters keep rising fast,
Unemployment, with hatchet-faced smirk,
        stalks our cities and towns.

Territory, status, and love, sing the birds,
*   are all that really matter.*
For a year, we've not been required to be home
        to anyone but ourselves –

tucked in this refuge, this large cradle
        holding us motionless in its frame.
Every room of the Thought House contains solitude.
        Its doors wait for us to enter.

III. THE CAVE OF MAKING
(in memoriam Roddy Lumsden)

For this study, and for others like it, the model
      is a book-lined room with a desk,
a chaise longue and a lifetime on government furlough.
      As unclocked self I occupy
this toehold on the universe; this nest; this eyrie
      overlooking a stubbly patch
of yard, overgrown eucalyptus, a garden shed;
      this retreat perfumed with incense
in which I try out lines, improvise on the guitar,
      fall asleep in my struggle for
understanding of the Francophone philosophers;
      or sit, sentry-like, at the desk,
on watch for truth, or beauty, or structure – glimpsing them
      distantly while a rack of cloud
unlimns in cornflower blue over neighbouring rooftops;
      this refuge in which I recline,
letting half-formed thoughts billow like crushed charcoal
      blown through fingers in neolithic caves,
or rattle like the last match in a soldier's matchbox.
      It seems that I've been sitting here
for most of a weird year, staring through window-shutters
      at light's varying gradations,
hearing blackbirds defend their fragile territories,
      the drills and circular saws of
those thankful to fill lockdown with DIY projects.
      And I have spent much of this time
teaching literature through a laptop screen to children,

or trying to. And though some days
they humour me, often it's like shouting in a cave
        to hear only the frail echo
of my own voice reverberating off the limestone.
        Sometimes, I'll sense you behind me,
sweet ghost, couched and supine, reading Brenda Shaughnessy,
        humming songs by Microdisney,
opening a beer or inventing the sevenling.
        I'll offer my apology
for not having made it to the hospice that last year,
        before you *quietly slipped out*
of Granusion into the Country of Unconcern;
        before the first lockdown; before
everywhere became a hospice, or a waiting-room.
        And though you are an awkward ghost
I sense you approve that I persist notwithstanding
        in this fey, unpopular art,
that I stubbornly insist upon obscurity,
        only to be read, sometimes, by
one who can rune. I know that you could, any moment,
        exchange my hospitality
to genially haunt a hundred other writers, but stay
        by my side until cocktail hour.
I've a new poem I want to run by you tonight.
        Its first resides in liminal.
Its second lies in turn. Third and fourth, a manuscript.
        In its end a poet's den.

IV. OUT THERE
(for Gareth Jones)

How, too, in these fragments of space, did the human being achieve
silence. How did he relish the very special silence of the various retreats
of solitary daydreaming.

GASTON BACHELARD

My father shoveled concrete from a tin bucket,
then levelled out foundations for the shed. That was
his last act I recall. He died. The shed dwindled.
It filled with crap we couldn't bear to chuck, burn, sell.
My mother held our roof-tree up alone; ignored
the shed. The first thing that I did when I acquired

a shed all of my own was paint it black, fit shelves,
a potting bench, a box of nested drawers. Hanging
from nails, a set of tools I clean and oil. Order.
A space from which this absent-minded goof can stare
into a garden on spring mornings when sunlight
illumines dewfall, spider webs, my coffee steam.

The loamy smell of compost, turps, bulbs stacked
in seedtrays under eaves. And so I grow sheddier
and beardier. I'll spend forever here, listen
to Adam Buxton's podcast while concocting
unnecessary woodwork projects with offcuts,
re-paint the rusting garden furniture, shout at

the city police helicopter. This awful year,

I've spent the hours in a deckchair by the shed,
read long-resisted books, grown squash; tried hard (but
    failed)
to filter out the ambulances' drone. Liminal,
a structure neither fully out nor in. Room for
a bike, some tins of paint, a baffled, midlife man.

V. UP THERE
(for the EU, which funded our loft insulation)

Just as Tom Thumb perched in the horse's ear, is
master of the force that pulls the steel ploughshare,
so – up there, among the dust and spiders – I
unearthed the yellowed newsprint from my mother's
private foolscap files, and gleaned historical
intrigue: a fire, insurance foiled, a court case.

Just as it is possible to imagine
an elephant emerging from a snail shell
yet inconceivable to ask, however
politely, if he'll go back in, so I once
disinterred strange secrets from a parental
loft, only to find they could not be put back.

Just as a dull childhood made me desirous
of scandal, intrigue, glamour, sin, and sent me
rummaging among the attic's totemic
bric-a-brac so, in midlife, I resist the
urge to keep anything in our loft at all –
just clear air between roof and insulation.

VI. THE GEOGRAPHY OF THE HOUSE
(for Andy Brown)

Every corner in a house, every angle in a room, every inch
of secluded space in which we like to hide, or withdraw
into ourselves, is a symbol of solitude for the imagination.

GASTON BACHELARD

While the flat we moved from
only had one privy,
now we make our choice of
        three within these walls.
And it's hard to over-
state the joy we find in
always having options
        when Dame Nature calls.

Now it doesn't matter
if I take a crossword,
magazine or notebook
        when I sit at stool.
Days might pass unnoticed
in that fertile nook where
poetry comes with each
        flicker of the soul.

Safe behind a jakes' door
we may dream at leisure –
neither work nor money
        hold dominion there.

Humans need oneiric
spaces and a shithouse
may fulfil the function
           of a dreamer's lair.

Ask a child to draw a
picture of a house and
if they add a doorknob
           to the front doorframe,
that shows that they know it's
more than just a construct –
it's a habitation,
           someone's human home.

If the same child's floorplan
makes space for a dunny,
I'd suggest you're dealing
           with a genius.
Which of us remembers
not to overlook the
washroom – architecture's
           unsung omphalos?

Guest rooms are essential,
but a sofa-bed can
make a front room double
           as a bedroom too.

Hosting friends and family,
we've learned to our cost that
xenia requires we've
         more than just one loo.

Auden once observed that
gnostics might have flourished
if it hadn't been for
         Bazelgette et al.
Rising from the Thames those
heady Great Stink perfumes
deepened our mistrust of
         the corporeal.

Now our cities' sewers
fill wastewater treatment
plants with CoV-2 cells from
         hospital and home.
And we're all connected,
mindful we're a civitas
every time we're seated
         on the porcelain throne.

VII. ENCOMIUM BALNEI
(for Rachael Boast)

while I know that for you
                    this room makes the difference
        between sufferance and comfort
offers balm for pain
                    makes each day doable
I can only guess
                    how deeply such rites
                            inform your work
        how each line must be carved and polished
like a slipper bath fashioned from volcanic limestone

                    for most a bathroom matters less
        and yet this year
                    even I have found
that drawing a bath
on a Saturday or Sunday afternoon
                    has no more to do with cleanliness
than pouring a dram
        has to do with slaking a thirst

        for Jane and me
these days
    a bath is a trip
                    I'll put on a record
    mix a pair of wee martinis
twist brushed-bronze mixer taps
                    over aromatic oils

in that warm amniotic caul

a space that's better shared
                              with just one preferred other
        neither the private ablutions
of the anglo-bourgeois bathroom
                                  nor the communal
        routines of the Roman thermae
suit so well as taking turns *in utero balnei*
        with one we love

                        talk's better here
to converse naked is to be more present
                        to be
        more alert to the niceties
of conversation
                        as steam rises
                                  between one perched
                on a lowered loo lid
                                  and one at soak
in a rich acoustic
                        born of vitreous china
                                  and ceramic tile

a sense of having withdrawn
                                  one step farther even
        than the relative withdrawal of
the rest of the house
                        of being at two removes from
        the filthy world's feckless clamour

nothing to do here but soak
and sip
and chat
and dream

the slow marination of the psyche
in a hot bath at day's end
has no more to do with
the sharp gush of a work-morning shower
than a bathroom
having its own bolt
being lockable from the inside
has to do with the rest of the house

and I aspire to fill ours with
a bronze and volcanic limestone slipper bath
or even
like some Chinese mandarins
commission a bathtub
made from
the shell of a huge mollusc
le grand bénitier

and as I dream of reclining
in a nacre-lined oyster
the size of a coffin
my wife is climbing from her shell
like Botticelli's Venus
only a shade pinker
her right hand screening her right breast

like an allegory of the fusion
                        of spirit
        and matter

                        and here's where you'll find me
her Hora of spring
                    a towel of the finest cotton
        spread in welcome
                        spread in homage
and as I embrace her in its folds
                        we learn again
        how *skin becomes border country*
how in each day's exile
                    from each other
                            we must come
        again
                to this small room
                            to meet

VIII. GRUB FIRST, THEN ETHICS

—BRECHT

(for Andrew Jamison)

But if we could resurrect
   the shade of Bertolt Brecht,
we'd have to explain that the kitchen,
today, is the front line of ethics:
never has it been so abundantly clear
   that our health, our future, the planet
      depends on what we do in here;
that our taste for the exotic, for a new ambrosia
   of braised pangolin or fruitbat *en croute*,
   threatens more than indigestion.
We've been caught red-handed roasting Thrinakian beef
   on our sun-spotted kitchen islands
and every ingredient, every tin,
   every box and sleeve of the packaging
is caught now in the shadow cast
   by our gustatory ideal of the citizen.

The ur-kitchen is Le Hollandais
in *The Cook, the Thief . . .* by Peter Greenaway,
   but while ours is not so sumptuous
   it's a temple to pleasure nonetheless,
where we perform our nightly sacraments
with oils and sauces, butter and cream.
      And even if it's invidious to evoke
gender in the preparation of a meal,
      it remains true that most nights Jane

[93]

can produce restaurant-grade plates
with minimal fuss; yet, when I take the hob
    I turn auteur, become possessed by
Michelin-style pretensions that require every pan
    in our possession, only to collapse
    like a failed soufflé when ravioli unglues,
        béchamel splits, filo pastry unwraps.

    I have done brioche and focaccia
        as an amateur midlife baker,
    though I never went so far as to ferment
        my own sourdough starter.
I live within half a mile of four *boulangeries*.
    Why compete with the professionals?
And I'm not looking to trade my red pen
and whiteboard for a *Bake Off* champion's apron
        and a new career in catering.
    Even if I were, in this part of Bristol
    this year, bread flour has sometimes been
        harder to come by than cocaine.
    No, I'm resolved: by far the best way
        to destroy what's fun
    about a kitchen would be having
        to make my living in one.

    And no room has mapped its function
        on a dream of conspicuous consumption
    more than the kitchen. But for those
    who can't afford a second mortgage
        in order to install a champagne fridge,

second oven, kettle tap, bifold doors,
the space retains its rustic charm: I made our shelving
    myself with twinslots and 18mm plyboard.
    This is not to eschew the Positive Way
for a thin-lipped scowl of pious negation.
The chef is today's philosopher monarch,
    our artist, priest, and politician,
the one we trust to deliver us from evil,
    and that brine should be the kingdom
        of salmon, tuna, octopus,
    is just one ingredient of her wisdom.

    This room entirely dedicated to
        the heir of the prehistoric barbecue
links us to history, to everything we've been;
and here, too, we're in the act of prepping what we'll be,
    like sous chefs in an unofficial
    clubhouse for the Anthropocene.
Here, where worldviews are made flesh
    we must be mindful of each other,
season each dish with a finely balanced blend
of sustenance and ethics, hospitality and pleasure –
    four essential spices you'd hope to find
    in any contemporary kitchen.
    Never more human than when we don
        an apron to cook, let us
    set the dial between the decadent
        and the parsimonious.

IX. FOR FRIENDS ONLY
(for David Clarke)

The lamp is the symbol of prolonged waiting.

GASTON BACHELARD

House prices in this part of town
preclude our having one room
to set aside solely for guests, so
we've no shrine to friendship
that sits empty most of the year
(correction: all of *this* year),

but three rooms do have a sofa-bed,
and you may freely choose
between one room that's lined with books,
one with records and hi-fi
and one that contains a Netflix-enabled tv.
It's not that we're inhospitable.

We know that a guest who reads
a room by the light
of a bedside lamp, at some point
leaves reading and returns imaginatively
to a room of their own history –
a happy one, we hope –

and we've allowed these rooms to fill
with curios, for the door
to a reverie of elsewhere must always

be left slightly ajar and,
just as in any stanza, the peculiar
transports more than the generic.

We're inhabitants of the houses of ourselves,
after all, but this year
it hasn't been just *distance and duties
dividing us*, and when something
becomes isolated too long it becomes round,
a thing concentrated on itself.

Now that we are emerging like hedgehogs
from a year of introversion,
will we find we've lost our fluency
in the language of friendship?
Will we find that roundness has forever
diminished something social in us?

A door may function as a symbol
of welcome, or of exclusion.
I am happy because coaltits
are building a nest in our garden,
but I'll be happier still
when I switch back on the beacon
of lamplight in our window.

X. TONIGHT AT SEVEN-THIRTY
(for Peter and Lynn Beudert)

Safe to assume
that no-one we know reserves
a dining-room
solely for dining. Auden's table of six
raconteurs
seems as dated as a suburban middle-class
high on sherry, hostess trolleys, pampas grass;
but that's never kept us from serving our share
of dapatical fare,
the cloop of corks, the convivial mix
of talented friends from every domain
of our lives; for we –
as all our guests will maintain –
love to throw a party.

And though it may
be censured now, the bash we threw
on our wedding day
brought eighty guests to this address.
A bacchic to-do –
sofa-beds removed to widen the dancefloor;
the kitchen replete with a buffet to diet for;
from a Vendéean cave, a small lake of wine;
a bathtub's worth of champagne
on ice (thanks to the Beudert largesse);
a playlist of songs curated to spotlight
a moment of dancefloor fame

for everyone; two who ended the night
in mild and hilarious shame.

At times like these
the house casts off sobriety
for licensed caprice,
becomes communal space, libertarian
territory.
Every guest meets on a mutual level
with a mutual premise. There's potential
for a comity of equal states.
A party makes us cognate,
briefly. A prude laughs with a vulgarian;
a bore is indulged, then deftly diverted
as a comic enlivens a sybarite;
the lonely make cause with the open-hearted;
the drunkard hides in plain sight.

That's the exemplar –
an ideal state whose founding depends
on who we are,
luck, timing, the booze we serve, the quality
of our friends.
And to play host to just one great soiree
is to walk in the shoes of Gatsby or Dalloway.
Fill the punchbowl, play the music loud,
step light through the crowd,
let "What you will!" be law among this polity.
For just one night, the house gives its all

to a higher idea of itself
than an asset, or shelter – the proprietorial
wilts in the heat of the commonwealth.

XI. THE CAVE OF NAKEDNESS
(for Byron Briggs)

Nearly 18,000 nights on earth, most of which (thankfully)
under roof tiles, yet never until now an insomniac. Three doors
  between here and the street, between me as citizen-worker
and me as unclocked self in pyjamas.
                              A book can be a door
  from that world in which I'm known by my state numbers
to the world I run through naked with Shadow and Anima.
  I read to translate myself from the Country of Consideration
into the Republic of the Unconscious,
                              only to awake again in the still hours.
Bed, wardrobe, chest of drawers, beside-table-cum-pharmakon.
Breathy snuffling from Jane. Byron's somnolent woofing
  as he dream-hunts huge rabbits through the Woodlands of Wish,
his back legs twitching away like a pack hound's in a zoetrope.
  And I'm struck again by the fierceness of my love
and the strong likelihood, given our relative ages, that I will
  outlive them both, that a time is coming when I'll wake
each night to find myself alone in the Kingdom of Grief.
                      Thank God for the day's distractions,
  how its business and bluster medicate unbearable probabilities,
how it somehow keeps the full weight of mortality
  floating in suspension – like a long-lived woman at swim in a lido,
deftly ploughing her daily lengths.
                              Only in the middle of the night
  do I get it whole, unmitigated. Its weight on my chest.
Only now, through self-pitying sighs, do I feel Byron's wet nose
  kiss my hand on the bed's edge and know the consolations

of his attentive ministry.
                         Meanwhile, the familiar ghosts
   crowd my bed – the same grievances and complaints; in unison
against me; something in their arguments, a logic I can't sweep away
   like crumbs from the duvet. Dawn's coming, a freight train,
and they've tied me to the rails – they're rubbing their hands with glee,
   prancing down the embankment in slapstick-villain hats and moustaches.
                         Our dreams may be unrepeatable
   to anyone other than a lover or analyst – for the symbol that knocks
at your door in a loud pink jacket, like a clownish uncle
   who won't stop reminding you he's your uncle, is less compelling,
somehow, than the symbolic charge, felt only with hindsight,
   of the naturalistic detail.
                         But what of insomnia's relentless motifs?
These anxious thoughts, uncoupled from all sense of proportion,
   that we must suffer alone till birdsong? Are these, too, unsayable?
In whom can we confide when yet another sleepless night
   in the cave beckons? The last crackling embers of a fire.
Night beasts calling out across the savannah under diffident stars.
                         Wolves sharpening their claws on the doorstep.

XII. THE COMMON LIFE
(for Jonathan Edwards)

As a child left alone in the house while mother
    worked to keep us, I'd pass time by
attempting to circumnavigate her front room
    without touching the floor;

a scrapling made mostly of hope and Vimto,
    I could inch along a shelf, the mantel
of a wall-mounted gas fireplace, a sideboard
    and (once we got central heating)

flatten one cheek to the wall while sidling crabwise
    along the top ledge of a radiator
without catastrophe. A house we've inhabited
    can never be merely an inert box.

As for how Frost/Grossman/Lemon would read
    my own living room 'through the keyhole',
I neither know nor care. Walls dressed with prints
    and paintings by friends and family,

shelves, sideboards, a mid-century coffee-table
    covered in books, records, magazines,
show us to be members of the clerisy, I guess.
    But this is a room we often move through

on our way to be productive elsewhere, to obey
　　our relentlessly clockable work ethic,
and it comes into its own only when we heed its call
　　to inertia, to idleness – a room reserved

not for doing, but for the quiet cultivation
　　of absolutely nothing in particular.
A room in which we needn't even be fully present
　　to each other, and sufficiently large

for companionable solitude. The living room
　　of a house should be like that of a hotel,
in which everyone is free to sit, read any old crap,
　　get gently wrecked in the afternoon

without the need to entertain its other occupants.
　　A room we may enter without knocking
and leave without curtain call. Large enough, if sociable
　　(and permitted to visit each other)

for guests to pair off in corners for tête-à-têtes
　　like characters in an Austen novel,
rather than take turns to perform
　　like lock-ins in a group chat on Zoom.

What other scale should we use to measure
　　a room than that of conviviality?
For though this one may be first and foremost
　　a geometrical object, *inhabited space*

transcends geometry. And we inhabit this space most
      when we do nothing at all; or, perhaps,
when small children are filling its every cubit
      with their boundless imaginations –

and though this may look, ostensibly, less like idleness
      than almost anything on earth,
it's really just a vigorous type of daydreaming
      (as reading and writing poetry

is a vigorous type of daydreaming).
      For what is a habitat, after all, but a shelter
for absent-mindedness – a refuge for those
      in exile from far *too much reality.*

Landscape with Knackered Barn

A country road ribboning the foothills
of a limestone escarpment – to the south,

low-slung December sun silhouetting
hedgerows of willow and dogwood.

Rusting gate. Knackered barn.
Windswept blackthorn. I am fifty years old,

driving home in a recent-model car,
and the view is enabling

a contentment I've not felt for decades
to germinate inside me, though I know

it's nothing more than a particular configuration
of sunlight and landscape and interiority

that mirrors a similar configuration
I experienced once as a child

in a field on the forest's edge I'd walked to
from our mundane housing estate –

before Death first knocked on our door
with institutional eyes – like those moments

in which the contingencies we inherit
as birth-right recede, and there we are,

lit up inside our own private dioramas.
I revelled in my escape from the estate,

at finding myself in an atavistic landscape
like those I'd pictured in the books

of my childhood reading, and I guess
that I must have attached that feeling

to what I'd found to hand around me –
a composition of low-slung December sun

silhouetting hedgerow, rusting gate,
knackered barn, windswept tree –

telling myself that if I banked this now
I'd be able to retrieve it in the future,

sometime when I most needed to,
after the thousand natural shocks etc.

It's not kismet. It doesn't mean anything.
Nothing more than a spider-thread linking

one flicker of consciousness across years
to another, causing this agreeable something

to happen inside me; yet, having wondered
so often if I'd make it even this far, for now,

driving this road to a home I almost think
I'd be content enough to live in till I die,

it's almost enough.

Afterword

The more I read and thought about it, *The Odyssey* seemed to be an elaborate conceit for the midlife experience. Carl Jung borrows a word from Heraclitus – *enantiodromia* – to signify a reversal of values in midlife, a shift from the ambitions of early adulthood towards a more inward-looking and reflective approach to the later stages of adulthood, and this idea seems to be encapsulated in Odysseus's transition from a hero of Troy to a lost, often bewildered, absent father and husband trying to find his way back home. But I found other aspects of the midlife experience there too, woven into the tapestry of this familiar tale. The *nostos* of the journey home; the complicated family relationships and the challenges of domestic love, or *storge*; the increasing incidence of the deaths of friends and family members, which engender a sharper sense of our own mortality and which, for Odysseus, manifest in an actual *katabasis* to the Land of the Dead; and, finally, the central theme of hospitality, the rituals of *xenia* that often define the moral quality of its characters – all of this, as I re-read *The Odyssey* in Emily Wilson's marvellous translation, seemed to rhyme with much of my thinking about my own midlife condition. I thought about proposing an Odyssey Complex as a middle-age counterpart to the neuroses of youth – an *Odyssey* Complex (rather than an *Odysseus* Complex) since these ideas needn't be the terrain of any particular gender. In finding these five key themes, I felt I'd been gifted a leather bag of tropes, something to help me navigate the turbulent seas of my midlife poetics. I hope that in these poems my reader, too, will find something to speed them on their way.

DAVID BRIGGS

May 2024

Acknowledgements

My gratitude goes to the editors of the following journals and magazines in which poems and articles from this collection (or earlier versions of them) first appeared. "Crackle (A-side)" and "Crackle (B-side)" in *Exclamat!on: An Interdisciplinary Journal*, vol. 5, July 2021. "Oak Galls" in *Raceme*, no. 10, autumn/winter 2021. An early version of "On the Pequod" appeared in *Poetry Wales*, vol. 56, no. 1, summer 2020, and an early version of "Transitions" was published in *The Sunday Tribune* (online), 1 August 2020. "Singing Along With Edith" in *Stride* (online), 31 March 2022. "Hemispheres" in *Museum Pieces: A Riptide Special Edition*, Dirt Die Press, 2023. "Landscape With Knackered Barn" in *Bad Lilies* (online), December 2023. The poems in the 'Habitat' sequence in the ξενία section were published as a pamphlet with Blueprint Press (2021). The collection was written to accompany my PhD thesis on midlife poetics, between September 2020 and March 2023. I am especially grateful to my supervisors, Professors Tim Kendall and Andy Brown, at the University of Exeter, for their insightful and fine-nibbed editorial assistance.

My reading of "Crackle (A-side)" was broadcast on West Wilts Radio for *The Poetry Place*, hosted by Dawn Gorman, in September 2021. I read "Crackle", "Cointreau" and "On the Pequod" at the Sixteenth International Novi Sad Literature Festival, Serbia, in September 2021 (online), and these poems were published in the festival's magazine. My reading of "On the Pequod" features on the *Poetry Wales* YouTube channel. My reading of "Static" appears on *The Poetry Archive*'s YouTube channel. "Praise" and "Genius Loci" were longlisted for the National Poetry Competition 2020.

This book has been typeset by
SALT PUBLISHING LIMITED
using Sabon, a font designed by Jan Tschichold
for the D. Stempel AG, Linotype and Monotype
Foundries. It has been manufactured using Holmen
Book Cream 65gsm paper, and printed and bound by
Clays Limited in Bungay, Suffolk, Great Britain.

CROMER
GREAT BRITAIN
MMXXIV